W9-CHQ-544

Discover
Japan

Susan Crean

PowerKiDS
press™

New York

Published in 2012 by The Rosen Publishing Group Inc.
29 East 21st Street, New York, NY 10010

Editor: Paul Manning
Designer: Paul Manning
Consultants: Rob Bowden and Professor Morris Rossabi,
   Distinguished Professor of History, City University of New York

Library of Congress Cataloging-in-Publication Data

Crean, Susan, 1970-
Discover Japan / by Susan Crean. — 1st ed.
     p. cm. — (Discover countries)
Includes index.
ISBN 978-1-4488-5269-7 (library binding)
1. Japan—Juvenile literature. I. Title.
DS806.C84 2012
952—dc22
                              2010046105

Photographs:
Cover l, Shutterstock/Allan Morrison; cover r, Shutterstock/Chai Kian Shin; 1,4, Shutterstock/Brian Weed; 3a,
Shutterstock/Johannes Compaan; 3b, Shutterstock/W.H. Chow; 3c, Shutterstock/Craig Hanson; 4 (map), Stefan Chabluk; 5,
Corbis/Jose Fuste Raga; 6, Shutterstock/Hiroshi Ichikawa; 7, Shutterstock/Frederic B.; 8, Corbis/Robert Gilhooly; 9, Corbis/Everett
Kennedy Brown; 10, Shutterstock/S.S. Guy; 11, Corbis/Blaine Harrington III; 12, Corbis/I.D.C; 13, Corbis/Everett Kennedy Brown;
14, Corbis/Toshiki Sawaguchi; 15, Shutterstock/Ian D. Walker; 16, Corbis/Bloomimage; 17t, Shutterstock/Mazzzur; 17b,
Corbis/Stefano Amantini; 18, Corbis/Stefano Amantini; 19, Corbis/T.W.Photo; 20, Corbis/Everett Kennedy Brown; 21, Honda;
24, Corbis/B.S.P.I.; 23t, Shutterstock/Peter Gordon; 23b, Shutterstock/Elena Blokhina; 24, Shutterstock/Norman Pogson; 25,
Shutterstock/Patrick Lin; 26, Shutterstock/J. Henning Buchholz; 27t, Shutterstock/Koi 88; 27b, Shutterstock/Manuel Fernandes;
28, Shutterstock/Neale Cousland; 29a, Corbis/Toshiyuki Aizawa.

All data in this book was researched in 2009 and has been collected from the latest sources available at that time.

Manufactured in China
CPSIA Compliance Information: Batch # WAS1102PK: For Further Information contact Rosen Publishing, New York, New York at 1-800-237-9932

Contents

Discovering Japan

Japan is an island nation in the North Pacific Ocean. It is made up of four main islands and more than 6,000 smaller ones forming an arc stretching for 1,500 miles (2,400 km). Japan's islands take up about the same land area as the state of Montana.

An Island Empire

About 450 of Japan's islands are inhabited. Most of the population live on the country's four main islands: Hokkaido, Honshu, Shikoku, and Kyushu. These four islands make up about 98 percent of Japan's total land area. Honshu is the largest of Japan's islands and contains the capital city, Tokyo.

Seclusion

For much of its history, Japan avoided contact with the outside world because it feared being dominated by foreign powers. That came to an end at the beginning of the twentieth century, when Japan became a powerful industrial nation and began to take over other countries, including Korea and Taiwan. In a short time, Japan built an empire similar to that of countries such as France and Britain.

In Japan, robes called kimonos are a traditional form of dress and are often worn on special occasions.

U.S. Influence

During World War II (1939–45), Japan fought on the side of Germany against the Allies. It was finally forced to surrender when U.S. forces dropped the first atomic bombs on the cities of Hiroshima and Nagasaki.

From 1945 until 1952, Japan was occupied, mainly by the United States. This was the only time in its history that another country has taken control of Japan. Many government and educational systems created after the war were influenced by the United States.

Modern Japan

Over the last 60 years, Japan has changed greatly. Today, it is one of the world's top manufacturing nations. It has the second-largest economy in the world, after the U.S.

Japan is a mix of old and new. It has the oldest monarchy in the world, yet it also has a modern parliament. It has many ancient buildings, as well as new skyscrapers. Many of its forests and mountain regions have been undisturbed for centuries, but in other areas, the spread of cities has transformed the landscape.

Japan Statistics

Area: 145,882 sq. miles (377,835 sq. km)

Capital city: Tokyo

Government type: Constitutional monarchy with a parliamentary government

Bordering countries: none

Currency: Yen ¥

Language: Japanese

DID YOU KNOW?

According to legend, Japan's founder, the Emperor Jimmu, was a direct descendant of the Sun goddess. The word *Nihon* (Japan) means literally "source of the sun."

◄ Japan's cities are large and densely populated. This is Ginza district in Tokyo City.

Landscape and Climate

Japan's islands are among the most unstable areas on the planet. Earthquakes, volcanic eruptions, and changes in sea level along Japan's coasts are all common. During the late summer and early fall, cyclones and typhoons are frequent in Japan, especially in the southwest.

Volcanoes

Japan is 80 percent mountainous. The country has 10 percent of the world's active volcanoes. It also has many dormant volcanoes. Mount Fuji, just west of Tokyo, is Japan's highest mountain. It last erupted in the early 1700s, but it is still considered an active volcano.

Facts at a Glance

Land area: 144,689 sq. miles (374,744 sq. km)

Water area: 1,193 sq. miles (3,091 sq. km)

Highest point: Mount Fuji, 12,388 ft. (3,776 m)

Lowest point: Hachiro-gata, –13.1 ft. (–4 m)

Longest river: Shinano, 228 miles (367 km)

Coastline: 18,486 miles (29,751 km)

▼ A terraced tea plantation in Shizuoka, with Mount Fuji in the background.

DID YOU KNOW?
Japan has more than 60 active volcanoes that are liable to erupt at any time. The country experiences more than 1,000 earthquake tremors each year.

Each of Japan's main islands has a mountainous central region, but long or continuous mountain ranges like the Pyrenees or Alps do not exist in Japan. Instead, Japan's mountains usually stand alone, surrounded by lowlands.

A Monsoon Climate

Japan has a temperate humid climate, and the seasons are governed by monsoon winds. The country's winter monsoon wind blows from late September to late March. It brings rain and snow to western Japan, and dry, windy weather to eastern Japan.

During the summer monsoon, from mid-April to early September, this effect is reversed. The summer monsoon brings warm temperatures and dry weather to western Japan and rain to eastern Japan. Throughout the year, it is warmer in the south than in the north.

Water Supply

Japan's monsoons bring heavy rainfall and create lush plant growth. But Japan still suffers from shortages of fresh water. This is because of the lack of lakes and other natural water reservoirs. Many rivers that flow through volcanic regions are acidic and their water is not suitable for drinking. In addition, building dams and reservoirs is difficult in mountain regions.

Japan has managed to dam some bays to create lakes such as Kasumiga-ura and Hamana on Honshu island. At 260 sq. miles (673 sq. km) Lake Biwa is the country's largest freshwater lake. It provides drinking water for 15 million people.

⬛ Steam rises from hot springs in a volcanic mountain region of Japan.

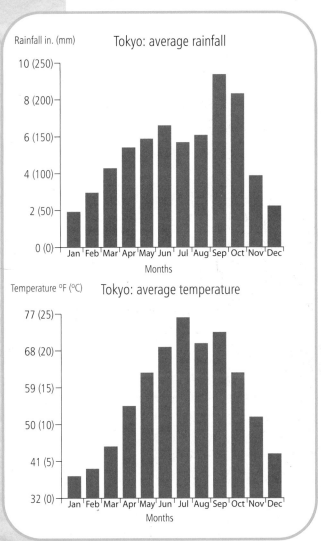

Rainfall in. (mm)   Tokyo: average rainfall

Months

Temperature °F (°C)   Tokyo: average temperature

Months

Population and Health

In 1912, Japan's population was 57 million. By 1940, it was more than 80 million, and since then it has grown to 127.1 million. Despite this rapid growth over the last 100 years, the country now has one of the slowest-growing populations in the world.

Japan's Ethnic Mix

Over the centuries, relatively few outsiders have settled in Japan, and only 1.5 percent of the people living in Japan are non-Japanese. The largest non-Japanese group are the Koreans, followed by the Chinese.

At the time of World War II, Korea was a Japanese colony. Many Koreans were forced to move to Japan to work for the Japanese war effort. In spite of being born and raised in Japan, ethnic Korean people living in Japan today do not have full Japanese citizenship and are classified as "resident aliens."

Facts at a Glance

Total population: 127.1 million
Life expectancy at birth: 82.1 years
Children dying before the age of five: 0.4 %
Ethnic composition: Japanese 98.5%, Koreans 0.5%, Chinese 0.4%, other 0.6%

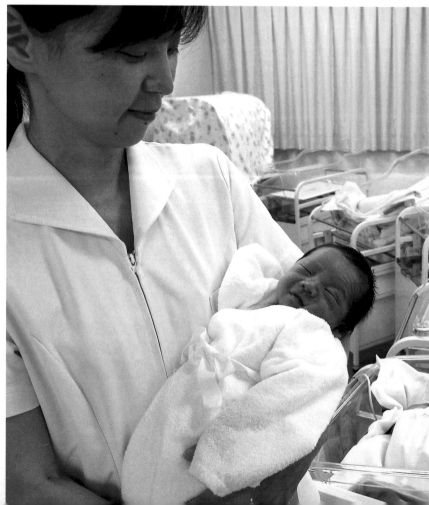

▶ A nurse holds a newborn baby at a maternity unit in a Tokyo hospital. Japan's birth rate is 7.64 births per 1,000—one of the lowest in the world.

Healthcare in Japan

Japan has one of the best state healthcare systems in the world. Infectious diseases such as malaria and TB have been brought under control by screening and by the use of vaccines. Japan still has many of the same health problems as the UK or the United States. Cancer and strokes are the leading causes of death in Japan, followed by traffic accidents and suicide.

Japanese people have a much lower rate of heart disease than people in the U.S. or the UK. Most experts agree that this is due to diet—either because the Japanese eat more fish and beans, or because they eat less fat and dairy products.

An Aging Population

In 2005, about 22 percent of Japanese people were 65 or older. By 2055, this figure is likely to be about 41 percent. The proportion of seniors in the population is growing because couples are having fewer children and are putting off starting a family until later in life.

One result of Japan's aging population is that people who are working have to pay more tax to support older people. This will put a great strain on Japan's economy in the coming years.

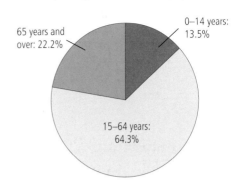

Japan: age structure of the population

65 years and over: 22.2%

0–14 years: 13.5%

15–64 years: 64.3%

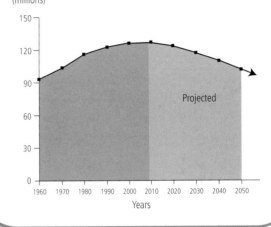

Japan: population growth, 1960–2050

Population (millions)

Projected

Years

▶ A therapist helps a senior recovering from a stroke at his home in eastern Japan. To reduce hospital costs, more and more elderly people are being cared for at home by visiting health workers.

Settlements and Living

In Japan, only about 18 percent of the land can be built on, so the population is squeezed into a small area. All Japan's major cities except Kyoto are situated in the narrow coastal plains of the four main islands.

Tokyo, Capital City

Tokyo replaced Kyoto as Japan's capital in 1868. Like London and New York, Tokyo is a global financial center. It is home to many investment banks and insurance companies. As well as being the administrative and political capital, it is also the center of Japan's transportation, broadcasting, and publishing industries.

Other Cities

Widespread urban growth began in Japan in the late 1800s. As Japan traded more with other countries, its ports grew. Cities along the coast such as Kobe, Yokohama, and Nagasaki ballooned in size.

For more than a century, Japan's industrial centers have continued to grow. Today Japan has 12 cities with populations of more than one million.

▶ With more than 35 million inhabitants, the Japanese capital Tokyo is the most populous city in the world.

Japanese Homes

In the cities, people live mostly in apartments. In rural areas, people live in larger, wooden-framed houses and are more likely to own their homes.

Most households only have four or five rooms and space is limited. To make the most of the space, rooms in Japanese homes are often multipurpose. A room can change from a sitting room, to a dining room, to a bedroom all in one day.

Rent or Buy?

Most Japanese people would prefer to own their own home rather than rent. However, because land is so scarce, property prices in cities are very high. Most people have to either rent an apartment or live on the outskirts of town where houses are cheaper.

Because of the shortage of affordable housing, many people find themselves with nowhere to live. In Tokyo's parks, there are "cities" of tents where homeless people shelter at night.

⬤ Traditional Japanese homes are sparsely furnished, with wooden floors, mats made of woven rice straw, and sliding paper screens instead of doors.

Facts at a Glance

Urban population: 66% (83.9 million)

Rural population: 34% (43.2 million)

Population of largest city: 35.3 million (Tokyo)

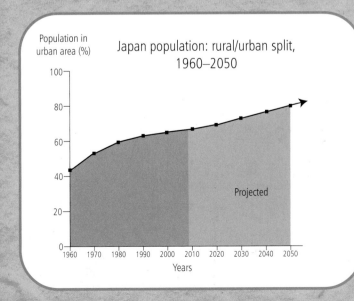

Japan population: rural/urban split, 1960–2050

Population in urban area (%)

Projected

Years

DID YOU KNOW?

According to a survey by a business magazine, Tokyo, Nagoya, Kobe, and Osaka are among the world's top ten most expensive cities in which to live.

Family Life

In the past, Japanese families were large, and three or more generations would all live together in the same house. In modern Japan, most families live in smaller units, and around 60 percent of households are nuclear families.

A Typical Family

As more people have moved to cities in search of a higher standard of living, larger families have been split up and nuclear families have become more common. Only 10 percent of Japanese households contain three generations of the same family. However, there is still a strong tradition of children, usually daughters, taking care of their parents when they are old.

Family Roles

Family life in Japan revolves around school and work. Men are usually the main money-earners, and women run the home and care for children and older family members.

More and more married women work outside the home, mostly in part-time jobs. In rural areas, women may work on the land or run the family farm while their partner is away earning money in the city.

▽ A young Japanese family enjoy a morning walk in the park.

Household Size

In the early 1950s, households with six or more people were common and it was rare for people in Japan to live alone. By 2005, the average household in Japan had only 2.6 people, and almost 20 percent of people in Japan now live alone. Many are older people whose children have moved away and who have lost their partner through death or divorce.

Living at Home

Japanese children often live at home for a long time. Most single adults live with their parents until they get married.

For men, this means living at home until they are over 28 years old, on average. Women usually get married when they are just over 26. Even after they get married, couples may decide to live with in-laws, although this is becoming less common.

Love and Marriage

In the past, marriages in Japan were arranged by the parents of the bride and groom, but "love matches" are becoming more popular. In a love match, a family friend or relative arranges a meeting between two single people. The couple then decide whether or not to take the relationship further.

⬟ A mother serves breakfast to her 20-year-old daughter on her "Coming of Age" day. Age 20 is considered the beginning of adulthood in Japan and is the minimum legal age for voting, drinking, and smoking.

Facts at a Glance

Average children per childbearing woman:
1.2

Average household size:
2.6 people

Religion and Beliefs

Japan has two main religions, Shinto and Buddhism. Followers of Shinto believe that everything in nature contains a sacred power called *kami*. Followers of Buddhism practice meditation in order to achieve inner harmony. Most Japanese people follow a mixture of the two religions.

Two Religions

Shinto religion has influenced Japanese life and thought for centuries. Its rituals are still regularly practiced by at least five million people. Many more visit Shinto places of worship and consider themselves Shinto followers.

Buddhism was introduced in Japan from Korea in the mid-sixth century CE. In the eighth century, Buddhism was adopted as Japan's official religion, and many Buddhist monasteries and temples were built throughout the country.

DID YOU KNOW?
Shinto originated in prehistoric times as a form of nature worship. Followers visited sacred sites to worship the sun, rock formations, trees, and even sounds.

▼ In Tokyo, crowds of business people gather outside a Shinto shrine to pray for prosperity and good health in the new year.

Shinto Shrines

Shinto places of worship are called shrines. A shrine has an inner hall where only priests may enter. Purity is important to Shinto followers, so keeping clean is a part of the religion.

There are about 80,000 shrines in Japan. Each shrine has a festival every year when people pay respects to kami and celebrate with food and drink. Shinto followers also make offerings of rice and tea on a special altar in their home.

"New Religions"

Some Japanese people follow so-called "new religions" that grew up in the late nineteenth century. The new religions are mostly rooted in Shinto and shamanism, but are also influenced by Buddhism and Christianity.

Christianity was introduced to Japan by Western missionaries, but less than 2 percent of Japanese people are practicing Christians.

Festivals and Celebrations

In Japan, the birth of a new baby is often celebrated with a visit to a Shinto shrine. Weddings are often performed by Shinto priests, but Christian weddings are also popular. Funerals are mostly conducted by Buddhist monks.

New Year's Eve is the biggest holiday of the year, and a favorite time for visiting shrines or temples. The Japanese also celebrate Japan's national holiday, the birthday of Emperor Akihito, on December 23 each year.

The entrance to Heian Jingu, a Shinto shrine in Kyoto built in honor of two former Japanese emperors.

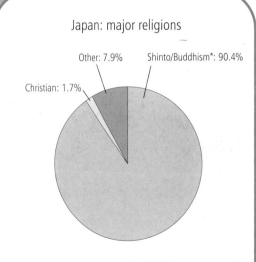

Japan: major religions

Other: 7.9%   Shinto/Buddhism*: 90.4%

Christian: 1.7%

*Officially, followers of Shinto and related beliefs represent 84.2% of the population; followers of Buddhism and related beliefs represent 73.6%. In practice, many Japanese people follow both religions.

Education and Learning

Most Japanese people take education very seriously, and Japan's literacy rate is the highest in the world. More than 90 percent of Japanese students finish secondary education and over 40 percent graduate from college.

The American Model

Japan's school system was introduced after World War II and is based on the American schooling system. All children must attend school for nine years, starting from the age of six.

Children go to elementary school for six years and middle school from ages 12 to 15. Students who pass their exams then go on to high school for three more years and college for four years.

A Day at Elementary School

At elementary school, Japanese children work hard at a wide range of subjects, from math and science to cooking and sewing skills, English, and IT. They are also taught traditional Japanese arts such as *shodo*, which involves writing with a brush and ink.

▶ At elementary school, Japanese children are given homework every day—even during summer vacation.

Japanese writing is made up of complicated symbols called characters that stand for spoken sounds. In elementary school, children have to learn 1,000 characters by heart.

Higher Education

In order to get a place at high school and college, students have to take a written entrance exam. Many parents send their children to *juku*, or "cram school," to prepare for their exams. Places are limited and competition is usually fierce.

Japan has more than 3 million students in 1,200 universities and junior colleges. About 25 percent of students attend public universities. The best public universities are the national University of Tokyo and University of Kyoto. However, private universities are also popular and offer a high standard of education for students who can afford to pay for their tuition.

Lifelong Learning

For the Japanese, education does not stop when you leave school. Adults see learning as a way to improve themselves and enrich their lives. Some schools in Japan are designed only for those age 45 and older. In addition, about 700,000 adults attend college-style lectures every year in Japan, on subjects from European history to traditional Japanese arts and crafts.

◔ In traditional Japanese culture, characters are hand-painted using a special brush and black ink.

DID YOU KNOW?
More than 75 percent of Japanese children and adults read manga comics. Manga publishing is big business in Japan, and manga comics are now popular all over the world.

▶ Adult learners practice the art of Japanese flower arrangement at a school in Kyoto.

Employment and Econom

Japan's skills in manufacturing made it one of the great economic success stories of the 1980s. However, like every country, Japan has been affected by global forces, including the most recent economic recession.

Boom and Bust

From the 1960s to the 1980s, Japan's economy grew rapidly and Japanese brands such as Toyota, Sony, and Panasonic became famous all around the world. Then, in the early 1990s, Japan entered a recession. Factories shut down, prices fell, and the economy shrank.

By 2007, the economy was back on track, but since 2008, Japan has been badly affected by the global economic downturn. It is now clear that the country has entered another period of unemployment and falling prices.

The Challenge Ahead

Japan's industry is efficient and its work force is highly skilled. But Japanese corporations face sharp competition from countries such as South Korea and Taiwan, where labor costs are lower. Another long-term problem is that Japan's work force is reducing and more money from taxes has to be spent on healthcare for senior citizens.

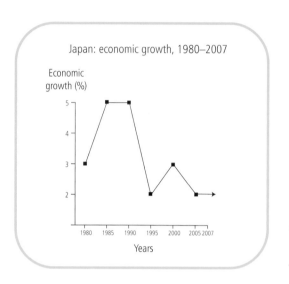

Japan: economic growth, 1980–2007

Economic growth (%)

Years

▶ Since the late 1980s, many Japanese women have joined the work force. Most are in part-time or nonpermanent jobs in the service sector. This girl works in a store selling tea.

The Job Market

Most Japanese workers—nearly 68 percent—are employed in businesses such as hotels, banks, and insurance companies, which serve customers, rather than producing finished goods.

Employees of Japan's big corporations are well paid, but are expected to work long hours and show high levels of loyalty. In the past, companies such as Honda and Nissan offered employees job security for life. Today, companies are employing more part-time workers to save money, and the future for full-time employees is much less certain.

Work, Work, Work

The Japanese working week is 44 hours—one of the longest of any country. Paid vacation time in Japan is about 18 days on average, but most people only claim about 8.5 days.

The Japanese dedication to work has been good for the economy, but not for family life. Many couples struggle to find the money for childcare to cover the long hours they spend at work. Some people say that Japanese couples are too busy working to think about having children, and that this is why the country's birth rate is so low.

Facts at a Glance

Contributions to GDP:
   agriculture: 1.4%
   industry: 26.4%
   services: 72.2%

Labor force:
   agriculture: 4.4%
   industry: 27.9%
   services: 67.7%

Female labor force:
   40.8% of total

Unemployment rate: 4.2%

▶ In 1990, the Tokyo Stock Exchange was the world's largest financial market, handling 60 percent of world trade in stocks and shares. It remains one of the big three financial institutions of its kind, alongside London and New York.

Industry and Trade

Japan has few natural resources of its own but depends on imports of raw materials to make high-quality products. It then takes these finished products and sells them to people in other countries.

Key Industries

Japan has some of the largest and most advanced factories in the world. It is a major producer of steel, rubber, aluminum, sulfuric acid, plastics, cement, pulp and paper, chemicals, petrochemicals, and textiles. It is also a leader in scientific research and is famous for pioneering the use of robots in manufacturing.

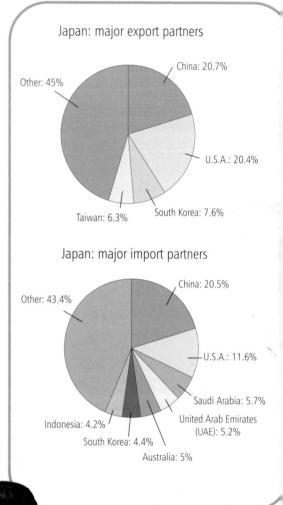

Japan: major export partners

- China: 20.7%
- U.S.A.: 20.4%
- South Korea: 7.6%
- Taiwan: 6.3%
- Other: 45%

Japan: major import partners

- China: 20.5%
- U.S.A.: 11.6%
- Saudi Arabia: 5.7%
- United Arab Emirates (UAE): 5.2%
- Australia: 5%
- South Korea: 4.4%
- Indonesia: 4.2%
- Other: 43.4%

◀ A worker assembles a Yamaha grand piano at the company's main factory in Kakegawa. As well as musical instruments, Yamaha produces a wide range of consumer goods from motorcycles to sports equipment.

In the 1990s, Japan's most important manufactured products were motor vehicles, machinery, and precision equipment, especially cameras. More recently it has produced some of the world's leading electronic products, including computers and telecommunications equipment.

Falling Exports

As a result of the global recession, prices of imported raw materials have gone up. At the same time, demand for Japanese products—particularly for cars and electronic goods—has gone down. Because of this, Japanese exporters are struggling, and many companies are being forced to lay off workers.

A Sustainable Future

As Japanese industry has expanded, the country's energy needs have grown. 78 percent of Japan's energy is supplied from abroad, and a large roportion of fossil fuels is imported.

One way Japan is trying to reduce energy imports is by relying less on oil and gasoline. Many people in Japan now drive hybrid cars, which save energy by running on a mixture of gas and electricity. Japan is also leading the way with many types of energy-efficient technologies, including trains that run on combined diesel and electric power.

◐ Designed to help people by performing simple household tasks, Honda's ASIMO robot resembles a small astronaut. The name stands for "Advanced Step in Innovative Mobility."

◑ Launched worldwide in 2001, the Toyota Prius was the world's first mass-produced hybrid vehicle. It is still one of the most successful hybrid cars on the market.

PRIUS
THE PROVEN LEADER IN HYBRID TECHNOLOGY

Farming and Food

In Japan, farmland is scarce, and every suitable patch of land is used for growing. Rice paddies occupy most of the countryside. Other fields are planted with wheat and barley in the fall, and with sweet potatoes, vegetables, and dry rice (a variety that can be grown with less water) in the summer.

Rice

Japan's main agricultural product is rice, and most rice eaten in Japan is home-grown. Since Japan has only 13 percent farmland, it cannot grow enough wheat, soybeans, or other major crops to feed all its people. In fact, Japan has one of the lowest rates of food self-sufficiency of all industrialized countries. This means that much of its food has to be imported from abroad.

Facts at a Glance

Farmland: 13% of total land area

Main agricultural exports: prepared food, animal, and vegetable materials

Main agricultural imports: pork, corn

Average daily calorie intake: 2,770 calories

In rural Japan, a farmer hangs ripened rice stalks to dry in the sun. Once dry, the stalks will be threshed to separate the edible grains from the rest of the plant.

Overfished

As an island nation, Japan has always depended on the sea as a source of food. Fish is an important part of the Japanese diet, and the Japanese eat 30 percent of all the fresh fish consumed worldwide.

Japan's appetite for fish is so great that it is seriously affecting the marine environment. Overfishing by factory ships has drastically reduced the number of fish in the seas around Japan. Environmentalists believe it also threatens fish stocks worldwide as other countries compete to supply the Japanese market.

○ Two men prepare tuna fish steaks at Tsukiji market in Tokyo. Tokyo's fish market is the biggest of its kind in the world.

Food in Japan

Traditionally, rice has been the most important food in Japan. A bowl of plain cooked rice is served with most Japanese meals. It is even eaten for breakfast mixed with a raw egg and soy sauce.

Noodles, seafood, and soybeans are other staples in the Japanese diet. *Sushi* is a small ball of rice topped with ingredients such as fish. *Sashimi* is sliced raw fish. *Nori* is a flattened seaweed that is sometimes wrapped around sushi to make rolls called *maki*.

○ Western versions of the Japanese delicacy sushi are now eaten all over the world.

Beef and Chicken

The Japanese eat many of the same foods as the U.S. and Europe. People in Japan only started to eat beef and chicken about 130 years ago, when the country began to develop more contact with the rest of the world. Today, Japan is one of the top ten consumers of beef and chicken worldwide.

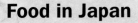

DID YOU KNOW? The Japanese do not use tables and chairs and silverware. Instead, they sit on cushions and eat from low tables, using chopsticks. The formal way to sit is *seiza* (kneeling).

Transportation and Communications

Japan has an excellent transportation infrastructure and was the first country to introduce the high-speed "bullet train." A single network of high-speed toll roads connects all Japan's major cities.

Getting Around

Japan has a highly developed and efficient railroad system. "Local" trains stop at every station; "rapid" trains skip some stations; express trains, called *kyuko*, stop at a few stations; "limited express" trains, called *tokkyu*, only stop at major stations. "Super express" or bullet trains, called *shinkansen*, connect Japan's major cities.

Facts at a Glance

Total roads: 743,781 miles (1.2 million km)

Paved roads: 589,744 miles (949,101 km)

Railroads: 14,586 miles (23,474 km)

Major airports: 48

Major ports: 10

▼ Japan's bullet train network is one of the busiest in the world. The Tokaido line carries 151 million passengers a year—more than any other high-speed line in the world.

DID YOU KNOW?
In 1964, Japan's first bullet train traveled at speeds of 130 mph (210 kph). Today's bullet trains reach top speeds of more than 186 mph (300 kph).

As well as the train network, buses serve smaller towns, the countryside, and national parks. Highway buses connect cities, too, and are about 20–50 percent cheaper than the trains.

Car and Bicycle

Most Japanese city-dwellers prefer to use public transportation than travel by car. Outside the big cities, however, people depend on cars to get around.

The national highway network is well maintained, but because so much of the country is mountainous, there are many areas that cannot be reached by road.

Travel by bicycle is common in both urban and rural areas. In Japan, 15 percent of trips taken to work are by bicycle.

Island Links

All Japan's main islands are linked by roads, bridges, and tunnels. Most smaller islands can be reached by ferry. At 33 miles (54 km) long, the Seikan Tunnel between the islands of Honshu and Hokkaido is the world's longest undersea railroad tunnel.

Communications

Japan has one of the most advanced communications systems in the world. Even remote villages deep in the mountains are linked by telephone landlines and cell phone networks.

The country also has one of the world's largest Internet-based economies and its population has the highest proportion of Internet users in the world.

● Honshu-Shikoku Bridge is part of a system of suspension bridges connecting the islands of Honshu and Shikoku across the Inland Sea of Japan.

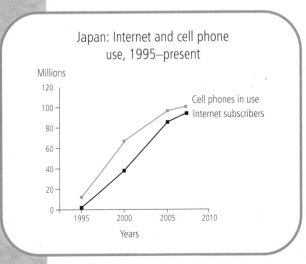

Japan: Internet and cell phone use, 1995–present

Leisure and Tourism

The Japanese like to be busy in their spare time. Sports and cultural pursuits are popular, and traditional martial arts such as such as judo, karate, and kendo (sword-fighting) still thrive in modern Japan.

Seeing the World

Japanese people travel widely within their own country and are knowledgeable about their own history and culture. Millions of Japanese people travel abroad each year, too. Favorite destinations include the U.S. West Coast, Europe, South Korea, and Hong Kong.

▼ Sumo wrestling is Japan's national sport. The aim is to use weight, strength, and skill to force your opponent off balance or out of the ring.

Facts at a Glance

Tourist arrivals (millions)

1995	3.3
2000	4.8
2005	6.7
2006	7.3
2007	8.3

DID YOU KNOW?

Sumo wrestlers train for years and live together in communal training "stables." Every detail of their lives, from what they eat to the clothes they wear, is dictated by strict tradition.

More than seven million foreigners visit Japan every year. Most are from South Korea, followed by China, Taiwan, and the United States.

Japanese Art Forms

Japan has many unique forms of art, including *haiku* (a form of poetry), *origami* (paper folding), and *ikebana* (flower arrangement). People also visit the many national parks and other types of parks and gardens in Japan, particularly when the cherry blossom is in flower. Gardens in Japan are seen as works of art, and garden design is as important as the design of buildings.

The theater is popular in Japan. *Noh* dramas are known for their use of masks and for dancing. *Kabuki* theater uses gesture and facial expression to communicate to an audience. *Bunraku*, or puppet theater, is another popular type of performance.

Karaoke is the singing of popular songs against recorded music. Karaoke started in Japan in the 1970s and is now a popular form of entertainment in clubs and bars around the world.

Sports and Other Activities

Popular outdoor activities in Japan include hiking, skiing, golf, swimming, baseball, tennis, and soccer. Indoor activities include *shogi* and *go* (strategic games similar to chess), the four-player game known as *mahjongg,* and table tennis.

⬤ Historic castles such as Matsumoto in Nagano are popular destinations for Japanese people and for tourists.

◗ Japanese taiko drumming is a spectacular mixture of rhythm, dance and high-energy display.

Environment and Wildlife

Japan has a rich but fragile natural environment that contains thousands of different plant and animal species. Many of these have been harmed by pollution from factories or by the rapid spread of Japan's cities.

Wildlife Populations

When Japan became an industrial country, its landscape changed dramatically. As animal habitats were destroyed, many species that were once common, such as the eastern white stork and crested ibis, died out completely.

As people in Japan became more aware of the danger of losing species, stricter laws were put in place to protect wildlife. Japan now has 28 national parks where landscapes and wildlife are conserved and protected.

Facts at a Glance

Proportion of area protected: 14%

Biodiversity (known species): 7,126

Threatened species: 116

Macaque monkeys are a species native to Japan. They live mostly in forests but can often be seen bathing in hot springs during the winter.

Whales

Whale meat is a popular food in Japan, but many whales—such as the humpback whale—are endangered species.

The hunting of whales for food was outlawed in 1989, but Japan still evades the ban. About 400 whales are killed every year for what the Japanese call "scientific research." Afterward, the meat is packaged and sold.

⬤ This white beluga whale is a popular attraction at the Sea Paradise aquarium in Hakkeijima, west of Tokyo.

Many countries criticize Japan for hunting whales, but the Japanese claim that whaling is an important part of their traditional way of life.

Fighting Pollution

Air and water quality in Japan have improved in recent years, but pollution from China has made acid rain more common in Japan. Air pollution also drifts from China over western Japan, where forests above 6,500 ft. (2,000 m) have been damaged. Eastern Japan, however, is less affected.

Since 1977, when Japan hosted the Kyoto Summit on global warming, the country has taken a strong lead on measures to protect the environment and cut greenhouse gas emissions. The recycling of cans and plastic bottles is well established in Japan, and many Japanese homes use solar power and other forms of clean energy.

DID YOU KNOW?
The Japanese islands are part of a major flyway for migrating birds and host more than 600 species, including cranes, herons, and songbirds.

Glossary

arable land suitable for growing crops

brand a product or service sold under a particular name

chopsticks short, tapered sticks used for eating Japanese food

climate normal weather conditions of an area

colony a country that is governed and run by another nation

culture the way of life and traditions of a particular group of people

cyclone a type of storm caused by circular air currents

dairy product a type of food derived from milk

delta a landform at the mouth of a river

dormant not active

economy the way that trade and money are controlled by a country

empire a group of countries controlled by a single, more powerful nation

export good or service that is sold to another country

extended family a family in which different generations live close together or under the same roof

fertile good for growing crops, especially in large quantities

GDP Gross Domestic Product: the total value of goods and services produced by a country

habitat the place, or type of place, where a plant or animal normally lives

import goods or service that is bought from another country

literacy being able to read and write

manga type of cartoon comic book popular in Japan

meditation clearing your mind of thoughts in order to feel calm and peaceful

monarchy a type of country ruled by a king or queen

monastery a religious community where monks live

monsoon a type of wind that brings rain when blowing from the southwest

natural resources raw materials such as wood and minerals that are found in a country

nuclear energy energy released by a nuclear reaction

nuclear family "core" family group, usually consisting of father, mother, and child(ren)

pharmaceuticals drugs used for medical treatment

precision equipment machinery that has to work very accurately

prefecture an administrative district in Japan

recession a period when businesses shut down, people lose their jobs, and the economy stops growing

reservoir a lake where water is stored

retail selling goods and products from a shop or store

rural to do with the countryside or agriculture

screening testing people's health to check for disease or infection

sector a division of something such as a type of industry

shamanism beliefs and practices involving contact with the spirit world

species a group of animals or plants that share common features

temperate a mild climate that is neither extremely hot nor extremely cold

textiles fabric or cloth

typhoon a type of tropical storm

unemployment being without paid work

urban to do with towns and town life

vaccine a medicine used to protect against an infectious disease

Topic Web

Use this topic web to explore Japanese themes
in different areas of your curriculum.

History
Research the Japanese empire to discover which countries were part of the empire during the 1900s.

Geography
Plan a journey through Japan's four main islands. Describe the different landscapes you would pass through and the types of transportation you might use.

Science
How does the shape of a bullet train help it to travel faster? What is this effect called? Draw a diagram to show how it works.

Math
The average Japanese home is 1,000 sq. ft. (100 sq. m), or 33 x 33 ft. (10 x 10 m). Measure the rooms in your own home. Is it larger or smaller than an average Japanese home?

Japan

English
A Japanese haiku has a pattern of five syllables, seven syllables, and five syllables. Write your own haiku following this pattern.

Citizenship
Do you think the way that Korean descendants are treated in Japan is fair? Write a letter to a Japanese citizen explaining your opinion and why you feel that way.

Design and Technology
Draw a design of what you think would be the perfect robot. Show what your robot would look like and write a brief description of what your robot could do.

IT
Imagine that you want to buy a video games console. Use the Internet to research five different brands. Then find out where the manufacturers are based.

Further Information, Web Sites, and Index

Further reading

A World Of Recipes: Japan by Julie McCulloch (Heinemann Raintree, 2009)
Welcome To My Country: Japan by Harlinah Whyte and Nicole Frank
  (Benchmark Books, 2010)
World In Focus: Focus On Japan by Celia Tidmarsh (Gareth Stevens Publishing, 2006)

Web Sites

Due to the changing nature of Internet links, PowerKids Press has developed an online list of Web sites related to the subject of this book. This site is updated regularly. Please use this link to access this list:
http://www.powerkidslinks.com/discovc/japan/

Index